DINOSAUR
ADVENTURES

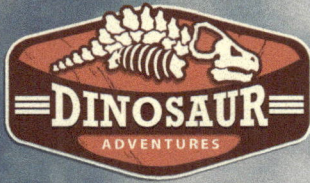

The Cretaceous Period

Ashley Lee

Explore other books at:
WWW.ENGAGEBOOKS.COM

VANCOUVER, B.C.

e→ WWW.ENGAGEBOOKS.COM

The Cretaceous Period Level 1
Lee, Ashley 1995
Text © 2021 Engage Books

Edited by: Alexis Roumanis and Lauren Dick

Image on page 18 by Luxquine
Image on page 22 by Nobu Tamura
Image on page 23 by Tim Evanson

Text set in Arial Regular.
Chapter headings set in Arial Black.

FIRST EDITION / FIRST PRINTING

LIBRARY AND ARCHIVES CANADA CATALOGUING IN PUBLICATION

Title: The Cretaceous period / Ashley Lee.
Names: Lee, Ashley, 1995- author.
Description: Series statement: Dinosaur adventures

Identifiers: Canadiana (print) 20210310111 | Canadiana (ebook) 2021031012X
ISBN 978-1-77476-494-7 (hardcover)
ISBN 978-1-77476-495-4 (softcover)
ISBN 978-1-77476-497-8 (pdf)
ISBN 978-1-77476-496-1 (epub)

Subjects:
LCSH: Readers
LCSH: Readers—Dinosaurs.
LCSH: Readers—Paleontology—Cretaceous.

Classification: LCC PE1117 .D56 2022 | DDC J428.6—DC23

Contents

What Is the Cretaceous Period?

The Cretaceous Period was the last time in Earth's history when dinosaurs ruled the planet.

4

It started about
145 million years
ago and ended about
65 million years ago.

What Were Cretaceous Dinosaurs?

There were two major groups of dinosaurs in the Cretaceous Period. Ornithischian (*or-nah-this-kee-an*) dinosaurs only ate plants. Their name means "bird-hipped."

Some saurischian (*saw-ris-kee-an*) dinosaurs ate meat and others ate plants. Their name means "lizard-hipped."

What Did Cretaceous Dinosaurs Look Like?

Many ornithischian dinosaurs had a horny beak.

Ornithischian hip bones pointed back towards their tails.

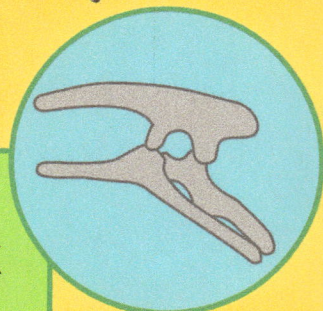

To help protect their eyes, saurischians had an "eyelid" bone above their eyes.

Saurischian hip bones pointed down and forward.

Where Did Cretaceous Dinosaurs Live?

In the early Cretaceous Period, most of Earth's land was close together. It slowly moved apart throughout the Period.

Asia

North America

Europe

Tethys Sea

Africa

Panthalassic Ocean

South America

Australia

Antarctica

Near the end of the Cretaceous Period, the land looked similar to how it does today.

Dinosaurs lived all over Earth in the late Cretaceous Period. Maiasaura (*my-ah-sore-ah*) lived in what is now America. Talarurus (*tal-ah-roo-rus*) lived in Mongolia. Ouranosaurus (*ooh-rah-noh-sore-us*) lived in Africa.

Arctic Ocean

Maiasaura

North America

Europe

Asia

Atlantic Ocean

Africa

Talarurus

Pacific Ocean

South America

Ouranosaurus

Southern Ocean

Antarctica

| 0 | 2,000 miles |
| 0 | 4,000 kilometers (km) |

N

Legend
Land
Ocean

Cretaceous Climate

The climate was very hot and sticky in the Cretaceous Period. There were many volcanic eruptions that caused wildfires.

The weather started to get cooler at the very end of the Cretaceous Period as ash and dust blocked out the Sun.

Cretaceous Plants

Flowering plants first appeared in the Cretaceous Period. The plants often grew fruit that held seeds.

Flowering plants are able to spread faster than non-flowering plants. They soon became the most common plants in the Period.

Cretaceous Ocean Life

Cretaceous oceans were ruled by the three largest ocean reptiles. These large reptiles ate sharks and bony fish called teleosts (*teh-lee-aasts*) to stay big.

The first of the three reptiles were called mosasaurs (*moh-suh-sores*). Some were about the size of a bus.

Ichthyosaurs (*ick-thee-oh-sores*) had large eyes that may have helped them see long distances.

The last of the three were plesiosaurs (*plee-see-uh-sores*). Long-necked plesiosaurs were slow swimmers. Short-necked plesiosaurs were fast swimmers.

Cretaceous Flying Creatures

There were many flying insects and early birds in the Cretaceous Period. There were also giant flying reptiles called pterosaurs (*teh-ruh-sores*).

Parvavis (*par-vai-vis*) birds lived at the end of the Cretaceous Period.

The largest flying animal of all time was a pterosaur called quetzalcoatlus (*kwet-sal-co-at-lus*). Their wings stretched to reach 36 feet (11 meters) from tip to tip.

Reptiles are cold-blooded animals. They use heat from the Sun to stay warm.

Kinds of Cretaceous Dinosaurs

The teeth of tyrannosaurus rex (*tie-ran-oh-sore-us reks*) were each 8 inches (20 centimeters) long.

Carnotaurus (*kar-noh-tore-us*) is thought to be one of the fastest dinosaurs ever.

The skull of triceratops (*try-serra-tops*) was one third of the size of its body.

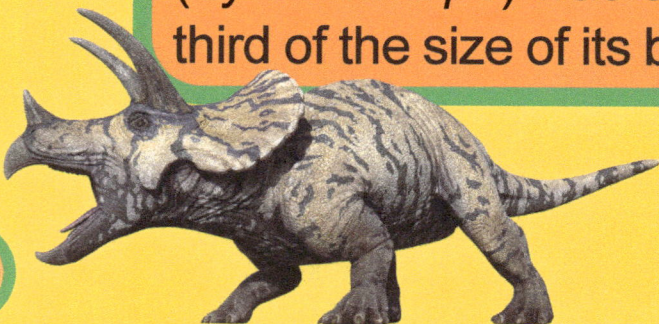

Spinosaurus
(*spine-oh-sore-us*)
is the largest known
meat-eating
dinosaur at 65 feet
(20 meters) long.

Velociraptors
(*vel-oss-ee-rap-tores*)
were covered in
feathers but their arms
were too short for flying.

Lambeosaurus
(*lam-bee-oh-sore-us*)
often lived in groups
called herds.

Curious Facts About the Cretaceous Period

Ants first appeared in the Cretaceous Period. They were not as common as they are today.

A giant frog called beelzebufo (*bee-el-zeh-boof-oh*) weighed 10 pounds (4.5 kilograms) and may have eaten small dinosaurs.

Sea levels were higher in the Cretaceous Period than any other time in history.

Grass appeared for the first time in the late Cretaceous Period. It was not a very common plant.

A small dinosaur called oryctodromeus (*or-ik-tow-drohm-ee-us*) made burrows underground.

The Rocky Mountains in North America were formed in the Cretaceous Period.

How Has the Cretaceous Period Impacted the World Today?

Flowering plants helped new insects such as bees, beetles, and butterflies to appear. Many of these early insects ate the pollen that flowers made.

Today, these animals help food grow for humans and other animals to eat. They do this by spreading pollen from male flowers to female flowers. This allows plants to multiply.

What Modern Animals Came From the Cretaceous Period?

The first marsupials appeared in the Cretaceous Period. Marsupials are animals with pouches on their bodies for carrying their babies.

Modern marsupials include kangaroos, koalas, and opossums. More than half of all marsupials live in Australia.

How Did the Cretaceous Period End?

Many scientists believe a meteor hit Earth about 65 million years ago. This caused volcanoes to erupt around the world and large dust clouds to block out the Sun.

Plants died without energy from the Sun. This meant plant-eating dinosaurs had no food and started to die. Meat-eating dinosaurs that ate plant-eating dinosaurs started to die too.

Quiz

Test your knowledge of the Cretaceous Period by answering the following questions. The questions are based on what you have read in this book. The answers are listed on the bottom of the next page.

1 When did the Cretaceous Period end?

2 What does saurischian mean?

3 Where did talarurus live?

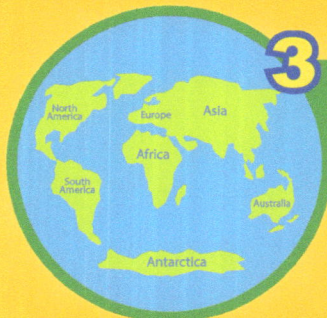

4 What helped bees, beetles, and butterflies to appear?

5 How long were the teeth of tyrannosaurus rex?

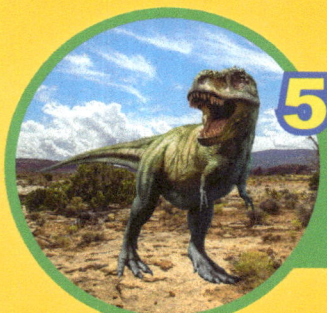

6 What are marsupials?

Explore Our Engage Books Readers!

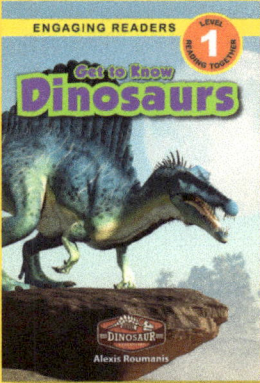

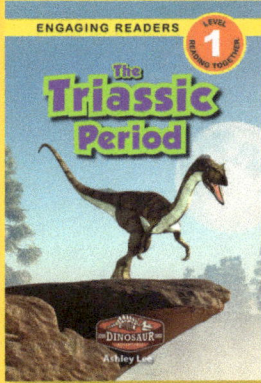

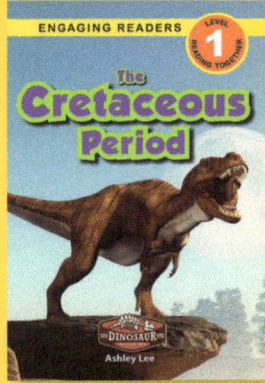

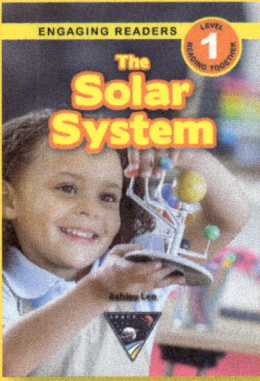

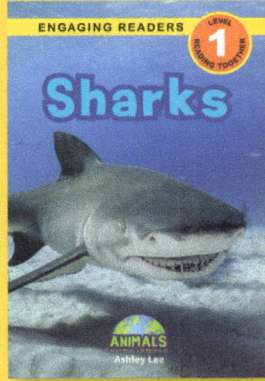

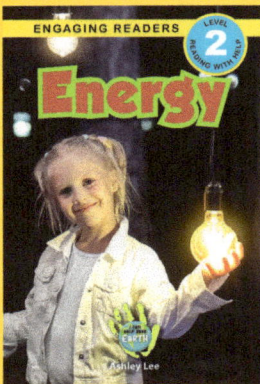

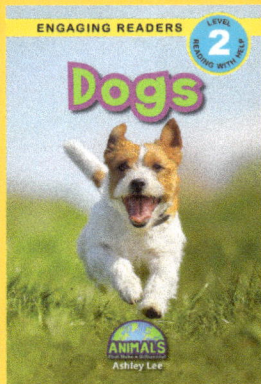

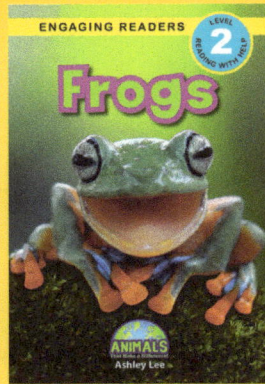

Visit www.engagebooks.com to explore more Engaging Readers.

Answers: 1. About 65 million years ago 2. Lizard-hipped 3. Mongolia 4. Flowering plants 5. 8 inches (20 centimeters) 6. Animals with pouches on their bodies